Siya Kolisi

Siyamthanda Kolisi, often simply referred to as Siya Kolisi, is indeed a trailblazing rugby icon with an inspiring story. Born on June 16, 1991, in Port Elizabeth, Eastern Cape, South Africa, Kolisi has risen to international prominence through his rugby career. His journey from a humble background to becoming the captain of the South Africa national team is an inspirational one.

Here are some key highlights and achievements in Siya Kolisi's career:

Rugby Career: Kolisi's rugby journey began at a young age, and he quickly rose through the ranks, showcasing his exceptional skills and work ethic. He played for several local teams in South Africa before making his way to the top-level professional leagues.

South Africa National Team: Siya Kolisi made his debut for the South African national team, commonly known as the Springboks, in 2013. His hard-hitting and dynamic style of play earned him a reputation as a formidable loose forward.

Captaincy: In 2018, Kolisi made history when he was named the captain of the Springboks. This appointment was significant not only for his leadership on the field but also because he became the first black player to lead the national team. It was a powerful symbol of transformation in South African rugby and a testament to his exceptional qualities as a leader.

2019 Rugby World Cup: One of the defining moments of Siya Kolisi's career came in 2019 when he led the Springboks to victory in the Rugby World Cup held in Japan. South Africa defeated England in the final to claim the title, and Kolisi's leadership and performance were crucial to this historic achievement.

Personal Story: Siya Kolisi's journey is marked by overcoming adversity. He grew up in a disadvantaged community and faced various challenges in his early life. His rise to rugby stardom has inspired many young athletes in South Africa and around the world.

Off the Field: Kolisi is not only a sports icon but also an advocate for social change and community development. He has been involved in various charitable initiatives and has used his platform to address important social issues, including issues related to racial inequality.

Siya Kolisi's impact extends far beyond the rugby field. He serves as a role model for aspiring athletes and stands as a symbol of hope and progress in a country with a complex history of racial divisions. His leadership, both in sports and in promoting social change, has earned him widespread respect and admiration.

Early Life

Siya Kolisi's early life is a testament to his resilience and determination. Growing up in the township of Zwide in Port Elizabeth, South Africa, he faced significant challenges, including the loss of his mother when he was just 15 years old. Despite these obstacles, Kolisi's talent and drive led to opportunities that would change the trajectory of his life.

Here are some key points from his early life and journey:

Early Challenges: Siya Kolisi was born to Phakama and Fezakele in Zwide, a township in Port Elizabeth. The loss of his mother at a young age was a tragic event that shaped his life and strengthened his resolve to succeed.

Scholarship Opportunity: At the age of 12, Siya's talents on the rugby field were noticed by scouts during a youth tournament in Mossel Bay. This led to a life-changing opportunity – a scholarship to attend Grey Junior School in Port Elizabeth. This scholarship was a pivotal moment in his life and provided access to quality education and rugby coaching.

Grey High School: Siya Kolisi's journey continued at Grey High School, an institution known for producing notable alumni in various sports, including cricket and rugby. He excelled as a member of the school's first XV rugby team, further showcasing his rugby talent.

Youth Rugby: After his time at Grey High School, Kolisi progressed through the ranks of youth rugby in South Africa. He was part of the Eastern Province Kings youth setup, participating in events such as the Under-16 Grant Khomo week and the Under-18 Craven Week, where the country's top young rugby talents compete.

Western Province: Siya Kolisi's journey in professional rugby continued as he joined Western Province, a top rugby team in South Africa. He continued to make a name for himself in the sport, demonstrating his exceptional skills and determination on the field.

Club Career

Siya Kolisi's club career is marked by his impressive rise through the ranks and his significant contributions to various teams in South African rugby. Here's an overview of his club career:

Debut with Western Province: Kolisi made his senior debut for Western Province in the Vodacom Cup in 2011. He quickly gained recognition for his talents and work ethic, which set him on a path to becoming a prominent figure in South African rugby.

Currie Cup Success: Kolisi's early years with Western Province included successful stints in the Currie Cup. He made 13 appearances and scored four tries, contributing to the team's success.

Move to the Stormers: In 2012, Siya Kolisi earned a place in the Stormers squad, a top South African Super Rugby franchise. He made an immediate impact, appearing in 16 matches and scoring a try. However, a thumb injury temporarily halted his progress, limiting his appearances in the 2012 Currie Cup.

Return to Form: Kolisi made a strong comeback in the following year, securing his spot in the Stormers' lineup. He faced tough competition in the loose forward positions but consistently delivered standout performances, which eventually led to his selection for the national team.

Leadership Roles: In 2017, Siya Kolisi's leadership journey began when he was appointed as the captain of the Stormers. This role allowed him to showcase his leadership qualities on and off the field. He would go on to make history when, on May 28, 2018, he was named the captain of the Springboks, the South African national team. This historic appointment made him the first black player to captain the Springboks in the team's long and storied history.

Move to the Sharks: In February 2021, Siya Kolisi made a significant move to the Sharks, a South African rugby franchise. This move followed a majority share purchase of the team by MVM Holdings. Kolisi's transfer to the Sharks marked a new chapter in his club career and continued his journey as a highly regarded player and leader in South African rugby.

Throughout his club career, Siya Kolisi's dedication, talent, and leadership qualities have made him a central figure in South African rugby and a symbol of inspiration for aspiring players from all backgrounds. His achievements with both his club and national teams have solidified his status as a rugby icon.

International Career

Siya Kolisi's international rugby career is indeed a remarkable story of talent, perseverance, and historic leadership. Here's an overview of his international career:

Debut and Early International Career: Siya Kolisi made his debut for the South African national team, the Springboks, on June 15, 2013, in a match against Scotland. His impressive performances quickly established him as a regular fixture in the national squad. Kolisi's dynamic style of play and versatility in the loose forward positions made him an invaluable asset to the team.

Rugby World Cup 2019: The pinnacle of Kolisi's international career came in 2019 when he captained the Springboks to victory in the Rugby World Cup. The tournament was held in Yokohama, Japan, and South Africa emerged as champions by defeating England 32–12 in the final. This victory marked South Africa's third Rugby World Cup win, tying them with New Zealand for the most tournament victories.

Historic Captaincy: Siya Kolisi's leadership as the captain of the Springboks was historic and significant for several reasons. He was not only the captain of the team but also the first black player to lead the South African national team. This milestone had a profound impact in a country with a complex history of racial divisions, and it symbolized transformation and unity in South African rugby.

Legacy and Inspiration: Siya Kolisi's role as captain and his ability to lead the Springboks to a World Cup victory left a lasting legacy. His leadership and success inspired countless individuals, particularly young athletes from underprivileged backgrounds, to pursue their dreams in the world of rugby and beyond.

Personal Life

Siya Kolisi's personal life is characterized by his commitment to family, faith, and his passion for various interests. Here are some key aspects of his personal life:

Marriage and Family: In 2016, Siya Kolisi married Rachel Kolisi, and the couple has two children, a son named Nicholas Siyamthanda (born in 2015) and a daughter named Keziah (born in 2017). Family plays a central role in Kolisi's life, and he often shares moments with his loved ones on social media.

Supporting Siblings: In a heartwarming gesture, Kolisi has also opened his heart and home to his half-siblings, Liyema and Liphelo. After spending five years in orphanages and foster care following their mother's passing, Kolisi welcomed them into his family, demonstrating his commitment to supporting his extended family.

Faith: Siya Kolisi is known for his strong Christian faith, which is a significant part of his life. He has been open about the role of faith in his personal journey and how it has guided him through various challenges and successes.

Sports Fandom: Apart from rugby, Kolisi is a passionate fan of English football club Liverpool F.C. His support for the club is well-documented, and he often shares his enthusiasm for Liverpool matches and events.

Alma Mater Honors: In recognition of Siya Kolisi's accomplishments and as a tribute to his legacy, Grey High School, his alma mater, renamed their first XV rugby field as "The Kolisi Field" in 2022. This gesture symbolizes the school's pride in his achievements and the inspiration he provides to current and future students.

Philanthropy

Siya Kolisi's impact extends beyond the rugby field. In response to the COVID-19 pandemic in South Africa, he and his wife launched The Kolisi Foundation in 2020. This foundation aims to address systemic issues in Gender-Based Violence, Food Insecurity, and Education and Sport, with a special focus on under-resourced areas such as Zwide township, where Kolisi grew up. Kolisi's philanthropic efforts have earned him recognition, including being named a UN Global Advocate for the Spotlight Initiative to eliminate violence against women and girls in July 2020.

With an impressive career, a heart dedicated to making a positive difference, and a legacy of breaking barriers, Siya Kolisi has left an indelible mark on the world of rugby and beyond. His story is one of resilience, determination, and the power of sports to inspire change.

Bibliography and Legacy

Beyond the rugby pitch, Siya Kolisi has shared his life story through his autobiographies. Jeremy Daniel's book, "Siya Kolisi: Against All Odds," and Siya Kolisi's own "Rise" offer readers a glimpse into his extraordinary journey, providing inspiration to those who aspire to overcome adversity and reach for greatness.

Siya Kolisi's legacy is not just one of personal achievement but also of breaking down barriers and paving the way for a more inclusive and diverse future in South African rugby. His historic captaincy and leadership have left an indelible mark on the sport, inspiring young athletes across the nation, regardless of their background, to dream big and aim high.

Test Match Records

Siya Kolisi's statistics on the international stage are a testament to his skill and dedication. His remarkable journey is marked by impressive victories, contributions, and milestones. As of August 7, 2022, Kolisi boasts an impressive win percentage, having achieved notable victories against teams like Argentina, Australia, England, and more. He has consistently been a crucial player, with a total of 35 tries scored in 67 appearances, showcasing his all-around rugby abilities.

Super Rugby Statistics

Throughout his Super Rugby career, Siya Kolisi demonstrated his skills and impact on the field. His performances have been consistent, with his tally of 19 tries scored over 116 appearances in Super Rugby. These figures reflect his dynamic contributions to his teams, reinforcing his reputation as a formidable force in the world of rugby.

Conclusion

Siyamthanda Kolisi, known simply as Siya Kolisi, has emerged as an icon in the world of rugby. His journey from the township of Zwide to becoming the captain of the Springboks is a testament to his talent, resilience, and determination. Not only has he left an indelible mark on the sport, but his philanthropic efforts and commitment to social change have further cemented his legacy.

Siya Kolisi's story is a true inspiration, a beacon of hope for those who face adversity, and a powerful reminder that with dedication and hard work, one can overcome the odds and achieve greatness. His impact on and off the rugby field will continue to resonate for generations to come, reminding us all of the transformative power of sport and the ability to break down barriers in the pursuit of a better future.

Continued Impact

Siya Kolisi's influence transcends the boundaries of sport and resonates far beyond the rugby field. As a role model, he has inspired countless individuals, especially young athletes, to believe in their potential and to work relentlessly towards their dreams. His journey from a challenging upbringing to achieving the highest honors in rugby serves as a source of motivation for many facing adversity.

Kolisi's commitment to philanthropy is a testament to his desire to make a tangible difference in the world. The Kolisi Foundation, founded by Siya and his wife Rachel, is dedicated to addressing critical issues in South Africa, from gender-based violence to food insecurity and education. By taking on these societal challenges, Siya Kolisi is not only a rugby hero but also a humanitarian who strives to make a positive impact on the lives of those who need it most.

Siya's appointment as a UN Global Advocate for the Spotlight Initiative to eliminate violence against women and girls underscores his commitment to global causes and his belief in the power of athletes to effect change beyond their respective sports.

Inspiring a New Generation

Siya Kolisi's success story is a beacon of hope, particularly for South Africa's youth. He has broken down racial barriers in a country where sport and politics have often been intertwined. His journey to becoming the first black captain of the Springboks and leading the team to a World Cup victory signifies a powerful shift towards inclusivity and unity in South African rugby.

Kolisi's life has shown that with determination, perseverance, and the unwavering support of a community, one can rise above life's challenges and reach the pinnacle of success. His story serves as an inspiration for those who face similar obstacles, showing them that it's possible to overcome adversity and shatter stereotypes.

Continuing Legacy

As Siya Kolisi's career and life continue to evolve, his legacy grows with each passing day. He remains a source of pride for South Africa, a symbol of what can be achieved through hard work and dedication. His contributions to rugby, his humanitarian efforts, and his commitment to making a positive difference in the world set a standard for the next generation of athletes and leaders.

Siya Kolisi's life and journey are a testament to the enduring power of sport to shape lives, uplift communities, and drive social change. His impact reaches far beyond the rugby pitch, and as he continues to inspire and lead, he solidifies his place as a true icon, both in South Africa and on the global stage.

A Bright Future

As Siya Kolisi continues to make history, his future remains bright and full of promise. His leadership and commitment to rugby, social change, and philanthropy show no signs of waning. With every match played, every charitable endeavor, and every inspiring speech, he cements his place as one of South Africa's most influential figures.

Kolisi's journey, from humble beginnings to global recognition, is a story of perseverance and hope that transcends borders. It's a testament to the power of sport to transform lives and create opportunities for those who dare to dream. His story is not only a South African success but a global example of the change that can be achieved through dedication and belief.

As we look ahead, we can only anticipate more extraordinary chapters in the life of Siya Kolisi. His impact will continue to be felt on the rugby field, in the hearts of those he inspires, and in the lives of the many he helps through his philanthropic efforts. The legacy of this remarkable athlete and humanitarian is far from complete, and we eagerly await the next inspiring chapter in the life of Siya Kolisi.

Siyamthanda Kolisi, better known as Siya Kolisi, is poised for a bright future that will be marked by his continued excellence in rugby, his impactful work in philanthropy, and his inspirational leadership. His remarkable journey, starting from a challenging upbringing to becoming a global icon, is a story of perseverance and hope that resonates with people around the world. Siya Kolisi's ongoing influence will extend to the rugby field, where he will undoubtedly achieve more milestones, as well as to the hearts of those he inspires and the lives of the individuals and communities he supports through his philanthropic endeavors.

As we look ahead to Siya Kolisi's future, we can anticipate many more remarkable chapters in his life. His impact is not limited to South Africa; it's a story that transcends borders and serves as an example of what can be achieved through unwavering dedication and belief in one's dreams. The legacy of this extraordinary athlete and humanitarian is far from complete, and we eagerly await the next inspiring chapter in the life of Siya Kolisi.

A Global Icon and a Beacon of Hope

Siya Kolisi's journey from a township in South Africa to becoming a global icon is a testament to the indomitable spirit of the human soul. He continues to be a symbol of perseverance and determination, inspiring countless individuals to pursue their dreams relentlessly. As he looks to the future, his legacy as a trailblazer in rugby and philanthropy is bound to continue making a profound impact.

In the realm of rugby, Siya's leadership, passion, and dedication will undoubtedly lead to more significant achievements. His name will be etched in the annals of rugby history, and his influence on the sport will be a source of inspiration for aspiring athletes worldwide.

Off the field, Kolisi's philanthropic efforts through The Kolisi Foundation will address critical social issues, striving to bring about lasting change in South Africa and beyond. His commitment to gender-based violence, food security, and education and sport is a testament to his desire to create a fairer and more equitable world.

As a UN Global Advocate for the Spotlight Initiative, Siya Kolisi's influence is not limited to the realm of rugby or his home country; it extends to the global stage. His voice, advocating for the elimination of violence against women and girls, is an essential part of the ongoing effort to create a more just and equitable world.

An Ongoing Inspiration

The story of Siya Kolisi is not just a sports success story; it is a beacon of hope and an ongoing source of inspiration for people from all walks of life. It exemplifies that no matter one's background or circumstances, with determination and resilience, greatness can be achieved.

As Siya Kolisi continues his journey, both on and off the rugby field, we can be certain that he will remain a symbol of excellence, leadership, and social responsibility. His legacy is one that will continue to motivate generations to come, proving that individuals can use their talents and success to create positive change in the world.

In conclusion, Siya Kolisi's life is an ongoing narrative of triumph over adversity and the enduring impact one individual can have on the world. His future is bound to be as extraordinary as his past, and his legacy will continue to inspire and uplift people, reminding us all of the transformative power of dedication and compassion.

A True Pioneer and Catalyst for Change

Siyamthanda Kolisi, or Siya Kolisi, remains a true pioneer in both the world of rugby and the realm of social change. His journey is one of transformation, not only for himself but also for those he touches through his actions and words. As we look forward to his future, we can expect that Siya Kolisi will continue to be a catalyst for positive change.

On the rugby field, Siya's leadership and athletic prowess are sure to result in more significant accomplishments. As a symbol of unity and diversity in South African rugby, he will inspire future generations of players, demonstrating that talent knows no boundaries. His influence will continue to shape the sport, breaking down barriers and ensuring that rugby remains a force for inclusion and progress.

Off the field, The Kolisi Foundation's impact is poised to grow, fostering positive change in South Africa and beyond. His commitment to addressing issues like gender-based violence, food insecurity, and education exemplifies his dedication to social justice. Through his advocacy as a UN Global Advocate for the Spotlight Initiative, Siya Kolisi's influence extends to the global stage, championing the cause of eliminating violence against women and girls.

An Eternal Source of Inspiration

The story of Siya Kolisi is not just a sports narrative; it is a beacon of hope, showing that adversity can be overcome through determination and resilience. It demonstrates that individuals can use their success and fame to create meaningful and lasting change in the world.

As Siya Kolisi embarks on the next phase of his remarkable journey, we can be certain that his life will continue to inspire, uplift, and set an example for individuals from all walks of life. His legacy is not just for today, but for future generations, reminding us of the profound impact one person can have when they use their talents and influence to make the world a better place.

In conclusion, Siya Kolisi's life story is a testament to the power of sport, leadership, and compassion. His future promises to be as extraordinary as his past, and his legacy will persist as a symbol of inspiration and positive change for all.

A Beacon of Hope for a Brighter Future

Siyamthanda Kolisi, known to the world as Siya Kolisi, stands as a beacon of hope for not only the world of rugby but for humanity as a whole. His journey, which began in the townships of South Africa, has led him to become a global icon, a trailblazer in sports, and a catalyst for positive change. As we peer into the horizon of Siya Kolisi's future, one thing is certain: he will continue to be a source of inspiration for generations to come.

On the rugby field, Siya's leadership, commitment, and undying passion for the sport will surely lead to more remarkable achievements. He has already left an indelible mark as the first black captain of the Springboks, and his influence on the game will only grow stronger. Young athletes worldwide will look up to him as a symbol of perseverance, unity, and the limitless potential of sport to break down barriers and bring people together.

Beyond rugby, Kolisi's journey is marked by his dedication to social change and philanthropy. The Kolisi Foundation, with its focus on gender-based violence, food security, and education, is a testament to his commitment to creating a fairer and more equitable world. His advocacy on the global stage, as a UN Global Advocate for the Spotlight Initiative, adds to his reputation as a champion for a better and more just world.

A Continuing Legacy of Triumph

The life story of Siya Kolisi is more than a sports success tale; it's an enduring narrative of triumph over adversity and a reminder that one person can create profound and lasting change. His journey from hardship to global recognition showcases the transformational power of determination and resilience.

As Siya Kolisi strides forward on his path, his legacy will remain a wellspring of inspiration and motivation for people of all ages and backgrounds. His future endeavors, whether on the rugby pitch, in his philanthropic work, or in advocating for social justice, are certain to make the world a better place. He will continue to exemplify the remarkable impact that one individual can have when they use their talents, success, and influence to create a more inclusive, compassionate, and just world.

In closing, the story of Siya Kolisi is a testament to the transformative power of sport, leadership, and social responsibility. His future is poised to be as remarkable as his past, and his legacy will persist as a shining example of inspiration and positive change for all.

A Champion of Unity and Progress

Siyamthanda Kolisi, affectionately known as Siya Kolisi, is not just an athlete; he's a symbol of hope, unity, and progress. His journey, which began in the heart of South Africa's townships, has taken him to the highest echelons of both rugby and humanitarian endeavors. As we look ahead to Siya Kolisi's future, we can be certain that he will continue to be a guiding light, leading the way for positive change.

On the rugby field, Siya Kolisi's journey is far from over. His leadership, unwavering commitment, and unwavering spirit will inevitably lead to more spectacular achievements. He has already made history as the first black captain of the Springboks, breaking down barriers and inspiring generations of athletes. Siya's influence in the world of rugby will continue to set an example of perseverance, unity, and the potential of sports to bring people together.

Beyond the realm of rugby, Kolisi's journey is marked by his tireless dedication to social change and philanthropy. The Kolisi Foundation, with its focus on gender-based violence, food security, and education, stands as a testament to his unwavering commitment to creating a more just and equitable world. His advocacy on the global stage, as a UN Global Advocate for the Spotlight Initiative, amplifies his voice as a champion for a better and more compassionate world.

An Everlasting Legacy of Inspiration

Siyamthanda Kolisi's life story is not just a sports success story; it's an enduring narrative of triumph over adversity, a shining example of what one person can achieve through determination and resilience.

As Siya Kolisi embarks on the next phase of his extraordinary journey, we can be certain that he will continue to inspire, motivate, and set an example for individuals from all walks of life. His legacy is not confined to the present but extends to future generations, reminding us of the incredible impact one individual can have when they use their talents, success, and influence to make the world a better place.

In conclusion, Siya Kolisi's life is a testament to the transformational power of sport, leadership, and compassion. His future promises to be as remarkable as his past, and his legacy will endure as a symbol of inspiration and positive change for all.

Printed in Great Britain
by Amazon

34357009R10020